THE
MEXICAN DAY
OF THE DEAD

AN ANTHOLOGY

COMPILED AND EDITED BY CHLOË SAYER

DESIGNED BY JULIAN ROTHENSTEIN

SHAMBHALA REDSTONE EDITIONS

BOSTON & LONDON

1994

Shambhala Publications, Inc.
300 Massachusetts Avenue
Boston, Massachusetts 02115
© 1990 by Julian Rothenstein
Introduction © 1990 by Chloë Sayer

Printed in China on acid-free paper ⊗

Distributed in the United States by Random House, Inc., and in Canada by Random
House of Canada Ltd
Library of Congress Cataloging-in-Publication Data
The Mexican day of the dead: an anthology/compiled and edited by Chloë Sayer.
p. cm.
Originally published as Mexico, the Day of the Dead.
ISBN 1-57062-026-1 (pbk.: acid-free paper)
1. All Souls' Day—Mexico.   2. Funeral rites and ceremonies—
Mexico.   3. Mexico—Social life and customs.   I. Sayer, Chloë.
GT4995.A1M49 1994   94-9617
394.2'64—dc20   CIP

The editor and publishers are grateful for permission to reproduce copyright
material from the following books:
FLOWER AND SONG, AZTEC POEMS, translated by Edward Kissam and Michael
Schmidt, *Anvil Press, 1977,* IDOLS BEHIND ALTARS by Anita Brenner, *Beacon
Press, USA, 1970.* Extracts from UNDER THE VOLCANO, DARK AS THE GRAVE
WHEREIN MY FRIEND IS LAID and SELECTED POEMS OF MALCOLM LOWRY by
arrangement with *The Peters, Fraser & Dunlop Group Ltd.* THE LABYRINTH OF
SOLITUDE: LIFE AND THOUGHT IN MEXICO by Octavio Paz, translated by
Lysander Kemp, *Allen Lane, The Penguin Press, 1967,* copyright ©
Grove Press Inc., 1961.

ACKNOWLEDGEMENTS

Chloë Sayer and Julian Rothenstein would like to thank Raúl Ortiz for help with this project. They are grateful also to Eduardo Llerenas, Marcela Ramírez, Trisha Ziff, Mariana Yampolsky and Faith Evans for encouragement and assistance. This book is affectionately dedicated to Elizabeth Carmichael.

INTRODUCTION

IN MEXICO the first and second of November belong to the dead. According to popular belief, the deceased have divine permission to visit friends and relatives on earth, and to share the pleasures of the living. To an outsider celebrations might seem macabre, but in Mexico death is considered to be a part of life. A familiar presence, it is portrayed with affection and humour by artists and craftworkers throughout the year.

Last Look. PHOTOGRAPH: MARIANA YAMPOLSKY

The modern view of death derives in part from that of pre-Hispanic times. For the Aztec, as for other ancient peoples, death signified not an end but a stage in a constant cycle. Just as day followed night and spring followed winter, so the continuity of life was ensured by sacrifice and by heroic death. Worship of death involved worship of life, while the skull — symbol of death — was a promise of resurrection.

Death was obsessively represented before the Conquest in stone, clay, gold and other materials. The gods were shown as ambivalent beings. Coatlicue, goddess of the earth and death, was portrayed with a necklace of human hearts, hands and a skull pendant. Two months in the Aztec calendar were devoted to the dead. Whereas the ninth month was dedicated to dead infants, the tenth included a great feast for dead adults.

The death of the individual was seen as a journey, for which numerous offerings were needed. The transition from life to death inspired many sad and haunting songs, composed by the Aztec élite. Included in this anthology, they describe life as a fleeting moment — a dream — from which death awakens us.

In Christian Europe, by contrast, death and the last judgement inspired horror and fear. Death was also seen as a journey, but the destination was either glory or eternal damnation. The 'dance of death', portrayed in medieval paintings and carvings, showed death as an equaliser, striking down both rich and poor, powerful and weak. The Spanish Conquest of 1521 brought about the fusion of Catholic atittudes and indigenous beliefs. In Mexico the Old-World fear of death diminished, while mortality ceased to suggest regeneration. Despite the passage of time, however, death is still seen as a journey by many Indian peoples. In Yucatán the Maya bury their deceased with food, drink, clothing and other elements for the journey to the place of the dead.

Today the theme of death motivates many craftworkers, who share the vision of Manuel Manilla and José Guadalupe Posada. Using skulls and skeletons, these gifted nineteenth-century engravers exposed the transitory nature of earthly pursuits, and ridiculed leading figures of the period. In modern times this purpose is served by the Linares family of Mexico City. Behind the bustling Sonora market, three generations fashion papier-mâché revolutionaries, postmen, fire-eaters and street-vendors of every type, all in the guise of skeletons. Similar ironic detachment is displayed by miniaturists in the cities of Oaxaca and Puebla. Here tiny skeleton footballers, wedding couples and priests hearing confession are modelled from clay and wire. Grimly humorous toys, often made for the festival of the dead, include clay skulls with movable lower jaws and cardboard skeletons that dance at the pull of a string. In Oaxaca small painted wooden theatres are peopled with rakish cotton-wool haired skeletons; as a handle is turned, one rises up in his coffin, while another raises a glass to his bony jaws.

Paper-cutters in the small town of San Salvador Huixcolotla, Puebla, spend much of the year preparing for the Day of the Dead. Artists such as Maurilio Rojas work with several sheets at once. Using a selection of sharp chisels to cut tissue or metallic paper, he hammers out skeleton dancers, mermaids and funerals watched over by angels. Because Maurilio also earns his living as a musician, skeleton rock singers with microphones join forces with Posada's *Catrina*. Great imagination is also shown by tinsmiths in Oaxaca City. Brightly painted tin suns, moons and purple rhinoceroses give way in November to jointed skeletons in brilliant colours.

Photography has a long history in Mexico. Until quite recently, it was customary to photograph dead children, or *angelitos* (little angels), in their best clothes. For most of the photographers included here, however, death is not seen as tragedy. In the words of Yolanda Andrade, 'It is ceremony, theatre and ritual'.

Celebrations vary from region to region, as does the timing of events. Everywhere the dead are welcomed with ceremony and respect. In the state of Puebla October 28 belongs to *los accidentados,* or those who die in accidents. The souls of dead children arrive on the 31st at midday; as they depart on November 1st (All Saints Day), their place is taken by the souls of dead adults. They, in their turn, withdraw at midday on All Souls Day, held since the thirteenth century on November 2nd.

Absent relatives frequently travel long distances to be with their families, for this is also a time of reunion for the living with the living. All over Mexico tombs are made tidy and adorned with flowers. Makeshift stalls in town such as Toluca sell sugar skulls and figures in the shape of guitars, sheep, angels and souls in purgatory. Bakers paint their windows with cavorting skeletons and skulls to advertise *los panes de muertos* (bread of the dead).

House altars, in towns and villages, are adorned with flowers, leaves and fruit; sometimes a path of flower petals from street to altar guides the returning souls. Elegant candlesticks and incense-burners are set out with offerings of food and drink. Care is taken to ensure that the aroma is strong, for it is the aroma or essence that the dead extract. On the morning of the second, families gather in the graveyard with more offerings. In some places brass bands serenade the dead with songs and music, while dances are performed in the Huasteca. No expense or effort is spared. The dead are never forgotten, because once a year they take their place beside the living to enjoy the fruits and flowers of the earth.

FURTHER READING:

Caso, Alfonso. THE AZTECS, PEOPLE OF THE SUN. *University of Oklahoma Press. Norman, 1958.*

Matos Moctezuma, Eduardo. MUERTE A FILO DE OBSIDIANA. Sepsetentas 190. *Mexico City, 1975.*

Matos Moctezuma, Eduardo *et al.* MICCAIHUITL: EL CULTO A LA MUERTE. Artes de México (Año XVIII, No. 145). *Mexico City, 1971.*

Museo Universitario de Ciencias y Artes. LA MUERTE: EXPRESIONES MEXICANAS DE UN ENIGMA. *Mexico City, 1974.*

Pomar, María Teresa. EL DÍA DE LOS MUERTOS: THE LIFE OF THE DEAD IN MEXICAN FOLK ART. (Exhibition catalogue). *Fort Worth, 1987.*

Oliver Vega, Beatriz. THE DAYS OF THE DEAD: A MEXICAN TRADITION. *Mexico City, 1988.*

Westheim, Paul. LA CALAVERA. *Biblioteca Era. Mexico City, 1971.*

FLOWER AND SONG:
ONLY A FLEETING INSTANT HERE . . .
AZTEC POEMS

Early Aztec history remains obscure. According to their own legends, however, they were the descendants of nomadic peoples from the north. By the time of the Spanish conquest of 1521, they had founded the great city of Tenochtitlan and established a vast empire. Although many Aztec songs were inspired by war, some were lyrical and philosophical. Composed by princes and priests, they mourned the ephemeral nature of life on earth. Part of a rich oral tradition, they were written down after the Conquest by Spanish chroniclers and preserved for posterity. The following poems are chiefly taken from CANTARES MEXICANOS, a twentieth-century anthology compiled by the scholar Angel María Garibay K. 'Flower and song' was the ancient Aztec metaphor for poetry.

1
Rejoice, rejoice
my flower king:
you own many jewels —

we do not come
  again:
only once
your heart knows the earth.

Xayacamachan, King of Huexotzingo circa 1510

13

2

It is not true that we live,
it is not true that we endure
on earth.
I must leave the beautiful flowers,
I must go in search of the mysterious realm!
Yet for a brief moment,
Let us make the fine songs ours.

Anonymous. Chalco

3

I, who cry and suffer,
am out of my head
Yes, I have this time, the present,
but I remember, and say

If I never died, if I were never to vanish . . .

I should go where there is no death,
where we could win some victory.

If I never died, if I never were to vanish . . .

Nezahualcóyotl, King of Texcoco, poet and orator. Circa 1459

4

We come but to sleep,
we come but to dream:
It is not true, it is not true,
that we come to live upon the earth.
Like the grass each spring
we are transformed:
our hearts grow green,
put forth their shoots.
Our body is a flower: it blossoms
and then it withers.

5

What am I to go with?
those flowers
which have closed?

Will my name be nothing some time?
Will I leave no thing behind me in the world?

At least flowers, at least songs!
How is my heart to work?

Perhaps we come, in vain, to live,
to come like springs upon dry earth.

Ayocuan

6

Our house on earth
we do not inhabit

only borrow it
briefly
        (be splendid, princes!)

here only
our heart sings
briefly, briefly
lent to one another

earth is not our last home:
take these flowers
        (be splendid, princes!)

Poems 1, 3, 5, 6 translated by Edward Kissam and Michael Schmidt.
Poems 2, 4 translated by Chloë Sayer.

FURTHER READING:
Garibay K., Angel María. POESIA NÁHUATL (3 vols)
(includes *Cantares Mexicanos*). *Mexico City, 1964.*
Flower and Song: AZTEC POEMS. Trans. by Edward Kissam and Michael Schmidt.
Anvil Press. London, 1977.

Mictlantecuhtli, pre-Hispanic lord of the underworld and god of death, from the Codex Borbonicus.

SOR JUANA INÉZ DE LA CRUZ

Although little known in the English-speaking world, the poetry of Sor Juana Inéz de la Cruz (1651-1695) is highly regarded in Mexico. An infant prodigy, she could read and write by the age of three; later she dreamed of adopting male dress and studying at University. Her intellectual powers attracted the attention of the Viceroy, however, and she became a lady in waiting at Court. In 1669 she entered a Jesuit order and became a nun.

She continued to study and to write for many years, until she was barred from these pursuits by her superiors. Today she is also admired as an early champion of women's education.

When Celia saw a rose with joyous face
All cheerfully suffused with pink and red,
Flaunting its beauty in some grassy place
And in vain splendour lifting up its head,
She said to it: Why should you fear to die,
Seeing that death can never take away
The smallest part of the felicity
Tomorrow that you have enjoyed today?
Although it closes quickly, your glad season,
Those days when you were vigorous and fair,
Take heed and listen to the voice of reason
And meet the approach of death without despair.
Fate will deal kindly with you, in your prime,
To spare you the indignities of time.

Most lovely rose, the flower of delight,
With subtle essence sweetening the air,
You teach, in purest hue of red or white,
A lesson for the beautiful to share.
What artist's industry can rival this,
Image of grace and charm without a plan,
Whose delicate being, all of idleness,
Dies sadly where its joyous life began?
How your proud time of splendour and display,
Of vanity and arrogant conceit,
Closes in misery, and in decay
Your beauty's shown as nothing but deceit!
So fading in the end you testify
By mute example even as you die.

Translated by John Paul Sayer.

EMBLEMS OF MORTALITY AND SUGAR SKULLS

EXTRACTS FROM THE LETTERS OF

FRANCES CALDERÓN DE LA BARCA

In 1821, after a decade of savage fighting, Mexico gained freedom from Spain. The time-span between Independence and Revolution lasted approximately ninety years and proved to be one of the best documented periods of Mexican life. Much information was provided by foreign observers such as Frances Calderón de la Barca, who spent two years in Mexico as the Scottish wife of the Spanish minister. Although living in the midst of revolts and ceasefires, she nevertheless found the time and the peace of mind to supply her correspondents in England with evocative word-pictures of customs in Mexico.

Her letters were published in 1843 with an enthusiastic preface by William Prescott. Written by 'a lady, whose position [in Mexico] made her intimately acquainted with its society', these letters were addressed 'to members of her own family and *really,* not intended originally, — however incredible the assertion, — for publication. Feeling a regret that such rich stores of instruction and amusement . . . should be reserved for the eyes of a few friends only, I strongly recommended that they should be given to the world.'

LETTER THE TWENTY-EIGHTH. SANTIAGO. NOVEMBER 3RD, 1840.

YESTERDAY, the second of November, a day which for eight centuries has been set apart in the Catholic Church for commemorating the dead, the day emphatically known as the *Día de Muertos,* the churches throughout all the republic of Mexico present a gloomy spectacle; darkened and hung with black cloth, while in the middle aisle is a coffin, covered also with black, and painted with skulls and other emblems of mortality. Everyone attends church in mourning, and considering the common lot of humanity, there is, perhaps, not one heart over the whole Catholic world, which is not wrung that day, in calling up the memory of the departed.

LETTER THE FORTY-SEVENTH. CITY OF MEXICO. NOVEMBER 4TH, 1841.

LAST SUNDAY was the festival of All Saints; on the evening of which day we walked out under the *portales* . . . to look at the illumination, and at the numerous booths filled with sugar skulls, etc., temptingly ranged in grinning rows, to the great edification of the children. In general there are crowds of well-dressed people on the occasion of this fête, but the evening was cold and disagreeable, and though there were a number of ladies, they were enveloped in shawls, and dispersed early. The old women at their booths, with their cracked voices, kept up the constant cry of 'skulls, *niñas,* skulls!' — but there were also animals done in sugar, of every species, enough to form specimens for a Noah's ark.

From: LIFE IN MEXICO. Frances Calderón de la Barza. *Chapman and Hall. London, 1843.*

Dead children, photographed at the turn of the century in Guanajuato by Romualdo García.

FEAST OF THE DEAD

FREDERICK STARR

Frederick Starr, the North-American ethnographer, made several study trips to Mexico towards the end of the last century. During one such trip he made a 'Collection of Objects illustrating the Folklore of Mexico' for the Folk-lore Society in London. This collection included a variety of sugar figures and a selection of 'ghastly toys' for the Feast of the Dead. The following information is from the accompanying catalogue.

Oct. 31 to Nov 2: Feast of the Dead. No festival of the year is celebrated with more gusto. We quote some notes made at various towns:

AGUAS CALIENTES:—

'Boys cut out skulls in cloth and attach them to a second piece, square and the size of the hand. With these they stamp designs in flour or chalk on backs. Others are pinned on to coats . . . Children ask for 'deaths.' . . . Early on a.m. of November 1, all go to church, carrying candles for the dead. Each is named, and prayer is made while they burn. The one to burn longest needed *most* prayer. . . . If a death in the house during the year, an open coffin is placed, and the bereaved sits over it and narrates his losses. A man happily remarried within a month, now *mourns* woefully, if never before. Crowds worship the dead priest.'

TEZONTEPEC:—

'Nov. 1st and 2nd, they set out offerings to the dead, consisting of an abundance of bread, fruit, dulces, wax candles, flowers. For grown persons they also place liquors, cigarettes, *mole, pulque, tamales.* Dogs are muzzled, so as not to molest the dead, who come to take the offerings. The doors of the place where the food is laid out are left open. Masses are said for the dead. The names of the parents are recited. On the last day of the feast the family and neighbours meet and eat and drink the offerings.'

PHOTOGRAPH: HUGO BREHME c. 1910.

MORELIA:—

'Servants say in the morning *'Mi muerto, Señor!'* and expect a 'dead', unless indeed the master is before them with the greeting . . . In the cemetery a line of tables is arranged along the wall, upon each of which is placed a skull and a bowl of holy water. On the tables the worshippers place their *reales* for prayers. The priest passes from table to table, sprinkling holy water and praying. Lights burn all day about the graves, and decorations are placed upon them. On the graves of priests are placed clothes and their portraits'.

JIMENEZ:—

'Nov. 2nd. People go out into the churchyard, carrying their house-hold ornaments and the bed or bedstead on which the dead died; this is ornamented with lace and curtains, white for children, black for grown persons. Those who have no beds take tables and place them over the grave. These they adorn with strips of paper, gold and silver paper stars, paper flowers, etc. The churchyard is crowded with smiling, gossiping people, who seem quite careless. Candles are burned at the graves. All sorts of refreshments are sold at the gates.'

From the CATALOGUE OF A COLLECTION OF OBJECTS ILLUSTRATING THE FOLKLORE OF MEXICO. *The British Folk-lore Society. London, 1899.*

CALAVERAS

JOSÉ GUADALUPE POSADA

Drawing of Posada by Diego Rivera.

Calaveras, or 'skulls', are witty epitaphs written for friends and celebrities while they are still alive. Often circulated on printed sheets during the Festival of the Dead, they provide an opportunity for political satire and comment. During the government of Porfirio Díaz, José Guadalupe Posada (1852–1913) became the master of the *Calavera.* Personalities and professions of the time were portrayed as skeletons and accompanied by humorous verses. Reproduced on the box lid is his most famous engraving — *la calavera catrina* — which shows a fashionable lady in the guise of a skeleton. Acclaimed after his death by such painters as Diego Rivera, José Guadalupe Posada continues to inspire Mexican artists and craftworkers.

GRAN
VERBENA DE CALAVERAS
EN EL PARQUE PORFIRIO DIAZ.

El Parque Porfirio Diaz
El mero dia de finados,
Estará de rechupete
Como jamás se ha mirado.
Gran verbena se prepara
Un lucido verbenazo
Donde verán calaveras
Toditos; pues ¡esta claro!
Verbena de calaveras,
Alegrona por demás,
Como ninguna se ha visto
Ni se habrá visto jamás.
Los panteones, desde luego
Sin un muerto quedarán,
Porque todos irán listos
A la gangota ¡caray!
¡Cuánto puesto! canillones!
Fruta y dulces sin contar,
Chacualole, pan de muerto,
Golletes, al por millar;
Magníficos barbacoas
Cacahuates... y la mar!
Sobre todo, mucha penca,
Curado como no hay más,
Que solo al verlo se trepa
Sin poderlo remediar.
Y respecto á diversiones,
Ninguna les faltará,

Esqueletos maromeros
Darán el salto mortal,
Y titeres y columpios,
Por todas partes habrá.
Varias músicas alegres
Buenas piezas tocarán
Con instrumentos de huesos
Y toditos bailarán
Patas arriba y sentados
Marcha fúnebre y cancán.
Aquello va á estar muy bueno
Magnífico, sin rival.
Es el gran dia de jolgorio
Que los muertos se darán,
Pues solo cada año comen
Y vuelo al hilacho dán.
El atracón será magno
Y la borrachera más,
Y habrá muchachas reguapas

¡Pues vaya si las habrá!
Con caras de calavera
Simpáticas por demás,
Todas pelando los dientes
Y prontas para bailar.
Novios habrá por montones,
Que en esto de enamorar,
Los muertos son muy picudos
Y habladores sin igual.
Las cuestiones y los pleitos
Vendrán como en natural,
Y allá van los canillazos
¡Y trompones pum! pum! prás!
Y aquello será un rebumbio
Del mismito Satanás.
Por aquí corre un esqueleto
Sin quijadas ¡ay! ay!! ay!!!
Por allá otro sin brazos,
Sin calaveras los más ......
Unos chillan, otros ladrán...
Résumen de lo ocurrido:
No se vayan á espantar:
Todos los muertos se mueren
Y aquí gloria y después paz.
Así se acaba el festejo
Y ya no hay más de que hablar....
Un responso y una cera
Y que les vaya muy ...mal!

Skeletons' fiesta in the Porfirio Diaz Park.

ESTA ES DE DON QUIJOTE LA PRIMERA,
LA SIN PAR LA GIGANTE CALAVERA.

A confesarse al punto el que no quiera
En pecado volverse calavera.

Sin miedo y sin respeto ni á los reyes
Este esqueleto cumplirá sus leyes.

Aqui está de Don Quijote
la calavera valiente,
dispuesta á armar un mitote
al que se le ponga enfrente.

Ni curas ni literatos,
ni letrados ni doctores,
escaparàn los señores
de que les dé malos ratos.

THE ONE AND ONLY, NEVER TO BE FORGOT
LARGER THAN LIFE CALAVERA OF DON QUIXOTE.

Repent your sins if you wish to save
Your soul from the torments of the grave.

Uncowed and unawed even by royalty
This skeleton will administer their justice with loyalty.

Here rides the cadaver
Of Don Quixote the knight,
Ready to take on
Any adversary in sight.

Neither doctors nor lawyers
Nor priests nor men of letters
Will escape the havoc
He wreaks on his betters.

28

EL GRAN PANTEON AMOROSO.

Leed, pues, este Panteón de los Amores
Todos los que habitáis aquí en la tierra,
Y hallaréis muchos gustos y dolores
Que el gran secreto de la tumba encierra.

Aquí van con sus amores
Gozando dos calaveras
La que en vida fué Dolores
Y él de apellido Contreras.

Aquí yace un buen torero,
Que murió de la aflicción
De ser mal banderillero,
Silbado en cada función;
Ha muerto de un revolcón
Que recibió en la trasera,
Y era tanta su tontera
Que en el sepulcro ya estaba
Y á los muertos los toreaba
Convertido en calavera.

General que fué de suerte
Y mil acciones ganó
Y sólo una la perdió
La que tuvo con la muerte.
Nadie hay que al mirarle acierte
Si fué un sabio ó de tontera,
Hoy es una calavera
Con gorro en verdad montado,
Y aunque esté condecorado
Hoy ya no es lo que antes era.

Aquí tienen á dos muertos,
Tal cual para cada quien,
Casados por desaciertos,
Paseando y vistiendo bien.

—¿Usted no sabe de amores?
—A según cuando conviene.
—¿Quiere ir conmigo á Dolores?
—Charrito, si aquí me tiene.

—Adios, no ande de celoso,
—Me cree con los ojos tuertos
—Si alguno me hiciera el oso
Se contaba entre los muertos.

—No quiero más amistad.
—Mi amor no ha sido quimera.
—Dejadme en la soledad
Y en paz, torpe calavera.

Y aquel charrito celoso
Pudo al fin tragar el queso,
Y con su muerte afanoso
Marchóse á llorar el hueso.

—Métale á la penca, vale.
—Atórele á los ardores.
—Ojos, pero no me jale
—Pos vamos para Dolores.

No he visto mujer más fina
Pa cantar una canción
Ni en habitito el Japón
Ni en toditita la China,
Pues canta la muy indina
Con tal aire y tal salero,
Que no hay en el mundo entero
Quien cante bien sus amores,
Como esta que vi en Dolores
Junto á un sepulcro ratero.

No me eche una rata muerta
Vestida de colorado,
El muerto chino tuimado
Que me ha espudo ya la puerta;
Mi calavera no es tuerta,
Y si canto sin quimera
Es hoy por la vez postrera,
Pues pronto la muerte flaca
Ya mero mis restos saca
Y á Dios de mi calavera.

—Con tal de llorar el hueso
Con usted, preciosa güera,
Me va á dar su copa y queso
Por muerto y por calavera.

México — Imprenta de Antonio Vanegas Arroyo, Calle de Santa Teresa número 1

The Great Pantheon of Lovers.

CALAVERAS DE CONFIANZA

QUE LES DARÁN  SU PITANZA

Aquí yace un gachupín
Que se llama Don Pedrito;
Que se murió de una *zorra*
Por meterle al chinguirito.

Marclalita la casera
Gastaba tanta dijera,
Que por no ocuparse en nada,
Se convirtió en calavera.

Una niña muy dengosa
Que se llama Mariquita
Y se viste de redrojos
Para parecer bonita
Por estúpida y grosera
La han vuelto ya calavera.

También los de Sucursales
Que siempre están cabeceando
O *apando* novelitas
Mientras *están* despachando.
La Muerte que *toco* acaba
Se los llevó del *zorongo*;
Y en Dolorcitos se encuentran
Comiendo mucho *mulango*.

Un bizcochero barbón
De Por San Pedro y San Pablo,
Se lo llevó el mismo diablo
Por grosero y regañón,
A sus marchantes espera
Convertido en calavera.

La costurera Chonita
De novios una docena
Juntó para distraerse,
Mas ellos que lo notaron
La hicieron *recalcura*.

Al actor D. Enriquito
Que aúlla al representar
Le han dado su calavera
De sílbidos y demás

En México Don José
Fue tan buto relojero,
Que descompuso relojes
Por subidísimo precio,
Como premio a su saber,
De los muertos en la fiesta,
Sus parroquianos amigos
Le volvieron calavera.

Los que *venden* estampillas
No se quedarán atrás,
Aunque siempre entreteniendo
A los que van á comprar,
Nos darán la calavera
Con mucha puntualidad,
Echando miel á los timbres
Para poderlos pegar
El billetero Don Juan
Todos los billetes fió,
Y ninguno le pagó
Aunque cobró con afán,
Por tan tarugo y tronera
Hoy le han hecho calavera.

Aquí duerme ya Moreno
Es comisario muy bueno
Más *bu un* que el *chacualole*
Y que los *pulques* y el mole,
A todos hizo *justicia*
Cual se debe, con *pericia*
Pero la Flaca implacable
A esta persona estimable
Como á otros lo mató,
Y Moreno se acabó.

Grabado de lo muy bueno
En México fue Posada,
Para grabar muertecitas
Tenía muchísima gracia,
E: use para "Dolores"
Dice: le tuvo más cuenta,
Y allí á los muertos les graba
A todos, sus calaveras.

Los carteros afanosos
Del Correo General
Por exactos y cumplidos,
En el servicio especial.

Una hedionda calavera
A todos les he de dar,
Comiéndose hasta los huesos
Porque muy buena ha de estar.

Los que empleados ahora están
En el Express Interoceánico
Son activos como pocos,
Tan activos como un ácido,
En premio á su buen manejo
Se les dará su *tstey*
Con sabrosa calavera
De buen dulce con panela

Los empleados del Express
Que se llama Nacional,
Por morosos y flojazos
A Dolores fueron ya
Allí al que no hay trabajo,
Y les dieron en su *cuerda*
Pues bultos ya no remiten
Que son sólo "calaveras

Ya murieron imperitérritos
Los autores celebérrimos
De las "Luces de los Ángeles"
Tan aplaudidos del público
Por su zarzuela pulquérrima
En sus sepulcros muy breve
Les pondrán por mausoleo,
De un turronero la estatua
Soñándose con los dedos.

Montado en su bicicleta
Pasó la vida Galván,
Inventando varios medios
Para mejor desaguar
Gastó plata á manos l*º*nas
Y era grande paseador,
Mas la "Flaca" inconsecuente
De pronto   lo *desaguó*

'Calaveras employed to serve, who will get what they deserve.'

Vignettes.

FURTHER READING:

JOSÉ GUADALUPE POSADA: ILUSTRADOR DE LA VIDA MEXICANA. *Fondo Editorial de la Plástica Mexicana. Mexico City, 1963.*
JOSÉ GUADALUPE POSADA: MESSENGER OF MORTALITY. *Redstone Press. London, 1989.*

SKELETON PRIESTS, PRESIDENTS AND POETS

EXTRACT FROM *IDOLS BEHIND ALTARS*

ANITA BRENNER

Anita Brenner, writer, translator and journalist, was born in Mexico in 1905. Although her family took refuge in Texas during the Mexican Revolution, she returned and lived in Mexico until her death in 1974. Her famous study of Mexican culture, IDOLS BEHIND ALTARS, was first published in 1929.

THE ANCIENT MEXICAN concern with death which created the messiah, remains like the messiah an organic part of Mexican thought. As a motif in art it springs from before the Conquest, cuts through the colonial period and appears over and over today. There are skulls in monolith of lava, miniature of gold and crystal, mask of obsidian and jade; skulls carved on walls, moulded upon pots, traced on scrolls, woven into garments; formalized into hieroglyphs, given a skeleton and an occupation in figurines; filled out around whistles, savings-banks, rattles, bells, holiday masks and jewels; woodcut and etched on ballads; strung into drinking-shop decorations; made into candles and toys. The skull has many meanings in Mexican argot. It trails gods, clowns, devils and subsidiary bogies in Mexican lore. There is a national holiday for it.

The Day of the Dead was fixed by the missionary friars according to the Christian calendar, but it was a habit long before. This holiday comes on the first and second of November. All Saints' Day is all adult ghosts' day, and All Souls' Day belongs to the children. The spirits return according to their ages, on the first and second eve, to dine with their living relatives. The table is set on an altar. There are beans, chili, tortillas, rice, fruit, other daily dishes, and the specialities of the season: pumpkins baked with sugar-cane, pulque or a bluish maize-brew with a delicate sugar film, and Dead Mens' Bread. For the children, candy skulls, pastry coffins, ribs and thigh-bones made of chocolate and frosted sugar, tombstones, wreaths, and pretentious funerals.

Pre-Hispanic pottery mask, half face with protruding tongue, and half skull, Tlatilco.

The living do not eat of the feast until the dead have left. They sit up all night 'with the little dead ones' (affectionate term for invisible human beings) as if at a wake — a Mexican wake; singing, praying, drinking, making a little love. And it is a wake, except that the prayers are said not for the dead, but to them. Everybody 'weeps the bone' picnicking in the graveyards. The tombs are turned into banquet tables similar to those at home. The food is put upon them, on banks of flowers, heavy purple wild blossoms and the yellow pungent cempoal-xochitl, ancient and sacred bloom. Little flags fly from the mounds; sometimes arcades and booths are raised over them, as upon holiday canoes. The recently bereaved or the especially punctilious really may shed a few tears for the honoured 'bone'. But somehow these tears are like the flowers and the skulls, simply part of the gesture. One's respected relatives, who 'have moved their sleeping mats' come to call. They must be treated courteously. A ceremonious gaiety is the proper tone.

Cosmopolitan Mexico City with its top layer of rice-powder faces is supposed to believe that the dead are only dust. Yet, carefully flavoured with doubt, the cultured Mexican tells many of the same tales the mule-driver has heard, tales of dead who appear, hold converse and depart, but always with nothing about them different from any other people. The Mexican ghost is no ha'ant. He calls out quietly from the grave to please tread lightly, as the earth is loose and drops unpleasantly upon him; or he enquires whether or no he may have a fresh jar of water, as he has used the other all up?

And why do the dead come back? Just to say hello, usually. Sometimes to see about a bit of business. The Mexican department of archaeology excavated at a spot which was pointed out to an Indian youth by the ghost of his ancestor, the prince Xicotencatl — and found a buried temple. The director of the national museum relates that once an Indian came to him and stated that in a hill near his village there lay an enormous treasure, one of the many that, it is said, were hidden from the lustful Spaniards. This Indian, an old man, said that he had come on the advice of the village priest. Leaving his name and address, he departed. Upon enquiry at the village the director learned that, indeed, such a man was of the place, but had been dead two years. The description given of the dead man fitted the visitor to the museum. He had been a charcoal burner. The hills where he had gathered wood were scoured for the supposed cache, but no treasure-cave was found. This is a story that the director tells with relish.

In Mexico City the at-home of November second becomes grotesquerie. Fashionable pastry-shops swing over French confections this urgent sign: Buy Your Dead Men's Bread Here. They turn their shining sophisticated displays into ranks and pyramids of skulls, miniature and life-size and bigger than that, lucent white, or creamy, with maraschino cherries for eyes and syrupy grins on their mouths, and rows of fine gold teeth. The funerals are of expensive milk chocolate, the wreaths of tiny candied fruits — and though this wonderful array is for the baby ghosts, no child in the city but awakes demanding on this day 'my funeral' or at the least 'my skull'.

The city cemeteries are as full of picnickers as the village graveyards. Automobiles and buses travel end on end all day, and in the cemetery itself there are lemonade stands, and tintype photographers making a splendid day on arm-in-arm lovers and family groups backed by a pretentious marble slab or a churrigueresque flower-arbour. Markets and parks fill out with the paraphernalia of carnival except that the eating-stands are delineated by an interminable row of enormous skulls, and are lighted by bier candles. Pottery, masks, figurines sold at this fair are not the useful, ornamental objects of other holidays. The figurines which throughout the rest of the year are realistic versions of people in all classes and professions, on Dead Men's Day appear stripped of worldly possessions such as flesh. The carpenter and the fruit-vendor, the priest and the scholar, the murderer, the poet and the prostitute, Don Juan and the president, the general, the cowboy, the sad Indian, the politician, the bullfighter, the aviator, the nun, the newsboy, the bob-haired steno and the foreign tourist take in skeleton form their usual places in the national scene — retaining, largely, the guitar-strumming, pulque-guzzling, and other pleasant bodily tendencies of plumper days.

Instead of ceremony, the city makes travesty. The press crystallizes an ever-present mood. It makes of itself a dead man's record, and so strong is the suggestion that even ordinary events appear invented or long past. One hardly knows, and one does not mind, the difference between dead and alive, past and present, fantasy and data. Special editions of comic publications publish political and theatrical caricatures of notables both dead and alive, together, all of them in skull and skeleton form, each

35

with an appropriate epitaph. A popular ballad which plays cleverly on this confusion sings, with the pretext of 'giving the newsboy his skull' the following reflections:

> He knows what he sells is lies,
> And all the news he releases
> The daily the dead man buys
> Tears into little pieces.
>
> This daily takes care to tell
> News of the opposite hue,
> It makes few bones and a smell
> Of all that the live men do.
>
> Black print in white is seen
> Truth appears out of lies,
> The fat man may turn quite lean
> And the live man usually dies.

This familiarity with death is shocking to the European. But where death is so much at home as in Mexico, he is no longer a dreaded and a flattered guest. The devil-may-care guerrilla mocks at him brutally. He sings, with a savage whoop and a pistol shot, 'If I am to die tomorrow, let them kill me right away! . . . ' The city jabs slyly at him, makes a clown of him. It belittles him for his trumped-up value. The Indian gives him the attention which he considers fitting. 'We all owe a tax to death,' he says. At the root of this is disbelief. Sufficient mourning and much respectful talk is partly something of the same obsequiousness the Aztecs had for their gods, and for the same reason. The concern is to control them. For the physical fact, a margin is made, wide enough for all its possibilities. Except as a physical phenomenon, death itself is disregarded.

It is no mood of futility that broods in this way over death, but rather a concern with death because of the passion for life. It is an artist's mood, his sense of limitation, his struggle with limitation, and his great assertion, the purpose of making — by his own strength — life. The control is achieved in the artist's way, by giving a physical place to a physical fact, making an image of it. The skull is the symbol of the thing which like the rain, the trees, the colours and the moving birds is caught, controlled, and made into lasting visible life. And it is the artist's way, as it is the Mexican way, to disregard other things for the sake of making images.

It is the thought of painters and sculptors, which travels from the eye and hand into abstraction. Thus the abstraction is in terms of movable, touchable, makable things. As: 'I, the singer, polished my noble new song like a shining emerald, I arranged it like the voice of a bird, I called to mind the essence of poetry, I set it in order like the chant of the zacuan bird, I mingled it with the beauty of the emerald, that I might make it appear like a rose bursting its bud, so that I might rejoice in the Cause of All.'

This is not thinking with words. Customs and traditions, laws and habits are 'the books or paintings of our ancestors;' descendants and successors 'the image and portraits' of their predecessors; the king is 'the eyes and mouth of the gods'; he is bidden guard 'the carved casket of wrought jewels' which is the nation. The human mind itself is fitted into an image, or into several, each of which may serve to symbolize some other thing; as for instance 'A sweet-voiced flower is my mind, a sweet-voiced flower is my drum . . . ' the flower being the Aztec synonym for abstract beauty. The most intangible affairs of the mind are shifted about likewise into different forms: 'Wonderful indeed is it how the living song descended upon my drum, how it loosened its plumes and spread abroad the songs of the Giver of Life . . . It rains down precious stones and beauteous plumes rather than words; it seems to be as one revelling in food, as one who truly knows the Giver of Life.'

So it is that, frequent as the skull, there is another motif, the human hand — an artist's symbol of creative life. From Aztec times to date, this motif appears, alone, or with an instrument, or holding the still significant flower. It is the Mexican answer to life, which is an answer to all the facts of it, including death. Over and over as in this typical poem, it is an artist's answer: 'I cried aloud, I looked about, I reflected how I might see the root of song, that I might plant it here on the earth, and that then it should make my soul to live.'

From: IDOLS BEHIND ALTARS, *re-published by the Beacon Press, 1970*

ANON.

POPULAR VERSES (19TH CENTURY)

Do you not hear the mournful knell
Nor heed the message of that bell?
Your breathless hurry's only waste:
You cannot win for all your haste.
Soon on the last bed where you lie,
The beauty gone from arm and thigh,
How then can you meet your lover
With only bare bones left to offer?

When I die, my dear,
Of my clay make a cup.
When you have thirst, from me drink.
The clay which clings to your lips
Is a kiss from your lover.

At the last, when life is done,
What lodging shall be given them
That wore the mitre and the crown,
The purple robe, the diadem?
What mansion will be found as good,
Fit equally for low and high,
For beauty and for noble blood,
Ugly and mean alike? Reply.
Only a sad grave where to lie.

Poems translated by John Paul Sayer

QUÉ VIVA MÉXICO!

SERGEI EISENSTEIN

All photographs in this section are by Grigori Alexandrov. Courtesy of the British Film Institute.

'Je ne fais pas du cinéma. Je fais du Mexique et du moi' (May 22, 1931)

Sergei Mikhailovich Eisenstein, the prodigious Soviet film artist, was born in 1898 in the city of Riga; he died soon after his fiftieth birthday in 1948. Although he is best known for the motion pictures he completed — STRIKE (1925), BATTLESHIP POTEMKIN (1925), OCTOBER (1927), THE GENERAL LINE (1929), ALEXANDER NEVSKY (1938) and IVAN THE TERRIBLE, PARTS I AND II (1944, 1948) — Eisenstein's most ambitious project and greatest personal tragedy centred on his unfinished film: QUÉ VIVA MÉXICO!

In 1929 the Soviet Union granted travel leave to Eisenstein, Grigori Alexandrov and the cameraman Eduard Tisse. From Europe they crossed to the USA, where they met Upton Sinclair, the left-wing novelist. Sinclair and his wife agreed to make themselves responsible for obtaining finance so that Eisenstein could film in Mexico; he in return signed a contract granting Sinclair and his associates ownership of future material. As Eisenstein travelled through Mexico, the shape of the film grew clearer in his mind. He planned to tell the story of Mexican civilization, from its beginnings through to 1931. The eventual structure, suggested by Anita Brenner's book IDOLS BEHIND ALTARS, was to feature four novellas, a prologue and an epilogue, with each part dedicated to a different artist.

Eisenstein's shooting script for the Epilogue was written on the stationery of the Regis Hotel in Mexico City (see p 49). Dedicated to Guadalupe Posada, it drew together various themes from the novellas and the Prologue, and included scenes for 'Calavera', the Day of the Dead. These scenes, with costumed skeletons in the Posada manner, were shot on the hotel roof, in between filming uniformed troops below for General Calles.

Eisenstein was fascinated by Mexico. According to Marie Seton, friend and biographer, it 'moved him more deeply than anything else in his life'. Among those struck by Eisenstein's energy and commitment was the journalist Morris Helprin. There was, he wrote, 'no rest while Eisenstein sees light in the skies. After eleven months . . . he is as active in his picture making as during the first days.' Eisenstein's endurance was not matched by that of Upton Sinclair, however. Relations became increasingly strained. When more than 170,000 feet had been shot, Sinclair withdrew his backing. Filming was suspended and Eisenstein returned to the Soviet Union. Despite his most desperate efforts, he never regained possession of the film footage. Edited in the USA, it was released as THUNDER OVER MEXICO. A short film called DEATH DAY was later compiled from the Epilogue.

Marie Seton has described Eisenstein's suffering and frustration. 'When I first met Eisenstein in 1932, shortly after he had heard that Sol Lesser was to arrange for the film's editing in Hollywood, he did not wish to go on living. He contemplated suicide and was only prevented by the loyal friendship of his cameraman, Tisse, and Pera Attasheva, then his secretary. He said he never wished to work in films again.' So great, apparently, was Eisenstein's anguish, that for two years he could not bring himself to speak about the Mexican film. Yet even in its truncated form, it has had a profound effect in Mexico itself. Films such as REDES, which espoused the cause of Indian peoples and showed up social injustice, were made under Eisenstein's influence. QUÉ VIVA MÉXICO! became the prototype for a whole generation of nationalist film-makers.

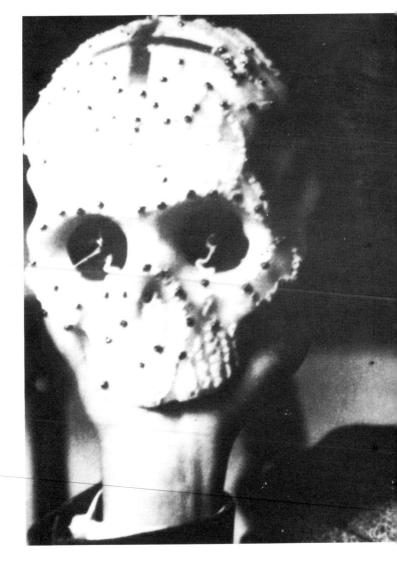

IN MEXICO the paths of life and death intersect in a visual way, as they do nowhere else; this meeting is inherent both with the tragic image of death trampling on life, and with the sumptuous image of life triumphing over death . . . The overlapping of birth and death . . . is visible at each step — in the cradle which is glimpsed inside every sarcophagus, in the rosebush growing at the summit of a crumbling pyramid, or in the fatal words that appear, half erased, on a sculpted skull: 'I was like you, you will be like me'. This impression is produced by the 'Day of the Dead' with its formal start, when the family, positioned on the tomb of the dead person and surrounded by candles, makes its funereal repast — all so that the young, on the very grave of their ancestors, can concern themselves when drunk with perpetuating their race. At every step life and death fuse constantly; so too do appearance and disappearance, death and birth. On the 'Day of the Dead' even small children stuff themselves with crystalized sugar skulls and chocolate coffins, and amuse themselves with toys in the form of skeletons. The Mexican despises death. Like all heroic peoples Mexicans despise death and those who do not despise it. Most important of all, the Mexican laughs at death. November 2nd, 'Death Day', is given over to irresistible mockery of death . . . And instead of a white wall of skulls, there is a bronze bas-relief of peons laughing.

Extract from Eisenstein's MEMOIRS translated by Chloë Sayer.

Скелетон облизывает

2ое Ноября
в Мексике
день
Мертвых

Диего
сфотографировано

Колокола
черная
Колокольни
траурные арки
женщины в черном
на коленях

Самолёт арки
женщины (индейские)
в белом
и черное (?) причём
ритм ...
свечи

пища внизе
хлебов, череп, кресты
стол с пищей
детский костюмчик
посажен на стул.
Родители справа
слева от костюма
Д.Т. вся семья за ранним
столом

разговор с покойником
на кладбище читают
процессия на кладбище
в чёрном
[на рассвете] молитвы
пища на
свечи. Молитвы.
Много народу и много
свечей.
черепа
маски черепов

Текст ритмически
разбивать цепочка
имитируя зубов.
чтение четкостью не соответствует
тексту

занавес падает

колокол
тусклый
череп

NOTES FOR FILMING THE EPILOGUE OF *QUÉ VIVA MEXICO!*
Dedicated to Posada.   17/XII—30
Skeleton introduces November 2nd, in Mexico—the Day of the Dead.

Skeletons (all) to be whitened with *priming* paint—eyes to be blackened
(perhaps with varnish)

Choose skulls of *primitives*—more character and disproportion in the faces.

The spoken text is rhythmically broken by a clacking of the teeth. (the
movement of the jaws should *not* correspond with the text.)

. . . the curtain falls . . . a bell . . . three candles . . . skull . . . belfry . . . funeral
arches . . . women in black—on their knees, etc.

setting up arches
women (Indian) in white and black (peon?)   } Diego [Rivera] *stylized*
candles
ritual food

food in the form of coffins, skulls, crosses
table set with food
child's costume placed on chair
parents on right and left of costume   } Interieur
long shot of whole family at long table
conversation with the dead from the same angle

solemn litany for the dead by the groups at cemetery in black (daybreak)
food on tombs . . . candles . . . praying . . . many people and many candles
. . . people more genre.

skulls and masks of skulls, alternating . . . more maskers . . . masker singing
portrait of Díaz (man beneath Díaz) [in cemetery]
maskers and in front of them . . . a corridor . . . Díaz calavera . . . maskers run by, laughing
Bishop [skeleton] . . . gentleman [skeleton] in top-hat
group laughs and sings . . . children dance in skull masks . . . faces on
tombs [these last two shots originally in reverse order] . . . children
chewing sugar skulls . . . paper streamers over saloon . . . playing with bones.
saloon. in front of it: calavera—general, bishop, top-hat [skeletons] kiss
one another . . . quarrel with bones . . . calavera—Zapatista [skeleton] . . . Lady [skeleton]
. . . toreador [skeleton] . . . embrace
calavera—groom and bride [from *Maguey* novella]
fight . . . lying on the tomb . . . Aztec skull (stone one, in museum) kiss . . . and [?]
skull (clay) . . . removal and murder of masks . . . after removal . . . stone . . . clay . . . masks
mask on naked infant . . . naked infant gurgles when mask is removed
. . . feet trample masks
infant shouts . . . life.

Translated by Jay Leyda

HOTEL REGIS

AVENIDA JUAREZ 77
MEXICO, D. F.

Posada

1) The toy-devils from the fair in
Guadalupe Hidalgo.

2) the Wallpainting on the pulcheria
in St Juan.

Callots Sensation
Daumiers Comet   } mention
Holbein's death dance
Goya (?) — denier!!

A last memo for the epilogue.

FURTHER READING:
QUÉ VIVA MÉXICO! Sergei Eisenstein and Ernest Lindgren. *Vision Press. London, 1951.*
IMMORAL MEMORIES Sergei Eisenstein. *Peter Owen. London, 1985.*
THE MAKING AND UNMAKING OF QUÉ VIVA MÉXICO! Edited by Harold H Geduld and Ronald Gottesman. *Thames and Hudson. London, 1970.*
SIGHT AND SOUND Jay Leyda. *Autumn 1958. London.*
EISENSTEIN AT WORK Jay Leyda and Zina Voynow. *Methuen. London, 1985.*

from *The Mexican Day of the Dead*

SHAMBHALA REDSTONE EDITIONS

from *The Mexican Day of the Dead*

SHAMBHALA REDSTONE EDITIONS

Painted papier-mâché skulls and death-masks made by the Linares family of Mexico City. Museum of Mankind, London. PHOTOGRAPHS: DAVID LAVENDER.

OVERLEAF: *Dream of a Sunday Afternoon in Alameda Park,* painted papier-mâché figures made by Miguel Linares and family in 1985. PHOTOGRAPH: DAVID WHARTON Courtesy of the Modern Art Museum of Fort Worth, Texas.

Hasta que la muerte los separe ('Till Death do them Part'). Painted clay wedding couple in a paper and reed prison, height 3 inches. PHOTOGRAPH: DAVID LAVENDER.

Skeleton horseman of painted clay in a wooden box,
height 2 inches. PHOTOGRAPH: DAVID LAVENDER.

PAGES 56/57: Xantolo dancers in Zapotitla, Hidalgo, during Day of the Dead festivities.
PHOTOGRAPH: CHLOË SAYER.

PAGES 58/59: Day of the Dead revellers in a Mexico City nightclub.
PHOTOGRAPH: ENIAC MARTINEZ.

PAGES 60/61: Child praying before the house altar.
PHOTOGRAPH: PABLO ORTIZ MONASTERIO.

House altar in Acatlán, Puebla. PHOTOGRAPH: LIBA TAYLOR.

Male Xantolo dancers dressed as women in Zapotitla, Hidalgo. PHOTOGRAPH: CHLOË SAYER.

Market stall in Mexico City. PHOTOGRAPH: ROBIN BATH.

Cross with flowers in Huaquechula, Puebla. PHOTOGRAPH: MARIANA YAMPOLSKY.

Floral cross and sugar skull for the departed. PHOTOGRAPH: PABLO ORTIZ MONASTERIO.

Diego Rivera in his studio in 1956.

Malcolm Lowry at Cuernavaca, June 1937.

FOR THE LOVE OF DYING

MALCOLM LOWRY

'Only against death does man cry out in vain . . . ' (Quotation from a letter written in 1946)

Malcolm Lowry began his life in Cheshire in 1909 and died in Sussex in 1957. Between school and university he went to sea, then met his first wife in Paris and moved to the USA. In 1936 on November 2nd — the Day of the Dead — he arrived in Mexico. UNDER THE VOLCANO, his finest and largely autobiographical novel, was set where he began it — in the small town of Cuernavaca. It was completed in Canada after eight years and four drafts. In 1945 he re-visited Mexico with his second wife, Margerie Bonner Lowry. During this trip he gathered material for another novel, DARK AS THE GRAVE WHEREIN MY FRIEND IS LAID. Deported in 1946 because of an unpaid fine, Lowry spent his last years in Canada, France and England.

UNDER THE VOLCANO is the keystone to Lowry's work. Published in 1947, it recounts the final day in the life of Geoffrey Firmin, British Consul and chronic alcoholic, on November 2nd 1938. Events are recalled in flashback exactly one year later. Afraid that circumstances might force him to change his title, Lowry noted: 'The Day of the Dead is my only alternative'.

The action in this tragi-comic novel is less external than internal; the Mexican landscape is an inner landscape. It is dense with symbols and with allusions to literature, religion and mythology. While in Mexico in 1945, Lowry received a letter from Jonathan Cape suggesting substantial revisions and cuts. His reply is one of the most remarkable literary documents of our time. Only after several readings, he argues, can the different layers of meaning become clear. The volcanoes, the Ferris wheel, vultures, a clockwork skeleton and a bar named *La Sepultura* (The Grave) are just some of the signposts along the road to impending doom. 'Life is a forest of symbols, as Baudelaire said, but I won't be told you can't see the wood for the trees here!', Lowry told his English publisher, who agreed to publish the manuscript in its entirety.

DARK AS THE GRAVE WHEREIN MY FRIEND IS LAID is based on Lowry's second period in Mexico. Sigbjørn Wilderness, who is clearly Lowry, has written a novel called THE VALLEY OF THE SHADOW OF DEATH. He has returned to Mexico with his wife, Primrose, to confront his past and to find his old friend, Juan Fernando Martínez. His journey is a descent which leads to the discovery that his old friend has been murdered and buried. The novel, unpublished in Lowry's lifetime, ends on a note of optimism. UNDER THE VOLCANO and DARK AS THE GRAVE were both conceived as part of a vast life-work — THE VOYAGE THAT NEVER ENDS.

UNDER THE VOLCANO
from Chapter 1.

TOWARDS SUNSET on the Day of the Dead in November 1939, two men in white flannels sat on the main terrace of the Casino drinking *anís*. They had been playing tennis, followed by billiards, and their rackets, rainproofed, screwed in their presses — the doctor's triangular, the other's quadrangular — lay on the parapet before them. As the procession winding from the cemetery down the hillside behind the hotel came closer the plangent sounds of their chanting were borne to the two men; they turned to watch the mourners, a little later to be visible only as the melancholy lights of their candles, circling among the distant trussed cornstalks. Dr Arturo Díaz Vigil pushed the bottle of Anís del Mono over to M. Jacques Laruelle, who now was leaning forward intently.

Slightly to the right and below them, below the gigantic red evening, whose reflection bled away in the deserted swimming pools scattered everywhere like so many mirages, lay the peace and sweetness of the town. It seemed peaceful enough where they were sitting. Only if one listened intently, as M. Laruelle was doing now, could one distinguish a remote confused sound — distinct yet somehow inseparable from the minute murmuring, the tintinnabulation of the mourners — as of singing, rising and falling, and a steady trampling — the bangs and cries of the *fiesta* that had been going on all day . . .

M. Laruelle finished his drink. He rose and went to the parapet; resting his hands one on each tennis racket, he gazed down and around him: the abandoned jai-alai courts, their bastions covered with grass, the dead tennis courts, the fountain, quite near in the centre of the hotel avenue, where a cactus farmer had reined up his horse to drink . . . What had happened just a year ago today seemed already to belong to a different age. One would have thought the horrors of the present would have swallowed it up like a drop of water. It was not so . . .

from Chapter 11 (towards the end of the book)

THE MOON had gone. A hot gust of wind blew in their faces and lightning blazed white and jagged in the north-east: thunder spoke, economically; a poised avalanche . . .

The path growing steeper inclined still further to their right and began to twist through scattered sentinels of trees, tall and lone, and enormous cactus, whose writhing innumerable spined hands, as the path turned, blocked the view on every side. It grew so dark it was surprising not to find blackest night in the world beyond.

Yet the sight that met their eyes as they emerged on the road was terrifying. The massed black clouds were still mounting the twilight sky. High above them, at a vast height, a dreadfully vast height, bodiless black birds, more like skeletons than birds, were drifting. Snowstorms drove along the summit of Ixtaccihuatl, obscuring it, while its mass was shrouded by cumulus. But the whole precipitous bulk of Popocatepetl seemed to be coming towards them, travelling with the clouds, leaning forward over the valley on whose side, thrown into relief by the curious melancholy light, shone one little rebellious hilltop with a tiny cemetery cut into it.

The cemetery was swarming with people visible only as their candle flames.

But suddenly it was as if a heliograph of lightning were stammering messages across the wild landscape; and they made out, frozen, the minute black and white figures themselves. And now, as they listened for the thunder, they heard them: soft cries and lamentations, wind-borne, wandering down to them. The mourners were chanting over the graves of their loved ones, playing guitars softly or praying. A sound like windbells, a ghostly tintinnabulation, reached their ears.

A titanic roar of thunder overwhelmed it, rolling down the valleys. The avalanche has started. Yet it had not overwhelmed the candle flames. There they still gleamed, undaunted, a few moving now in procession. Some of the mourners were filing off down the hillside.

Yvonne felt with gratitude the hard road beneath her feet. The lights of the Hotel y Restaurant El Popo sprang up. Over a garage next door an electric sign was stabbing: *Euzkadi.* A radio somewhere was playing hot music at an incredible speed.

American cars stood outside the restaurant ranged before the cul-de-sac at the edge of the jungle, giving the place something of the with-drawn, waiting character that pertains to a border at night, and a border of sorts there was, not far from here, where the ravine, bridged to the right on the outskirts of the old capital, marked the state line.

———◆◆◆———

DARK AS THE GRAVE WHEREIN MY FRIEND IS LAID
from Chapter 12.

MURIÓ in Villahermosa. The beautiful city . . .

Where had Fernando been buried? A longing to see his grave, to say a prayer there, overcame Sigbjørn. One day on the way back from a waterfall in Cuernavaca, they had decided to go to a cemetery. One part was very garish and full of blue and other coloured monuments and great trees and flowers, next to it a pitiful one, hot and dusty with only poor wooden crosses . . . In the fine cemetery Primrose was fascinated by a sort of shining crypt made of blue and white bathroom tiles, large as a room, with open walls, ceiling tiled, and at the back a sort of cache,

72

glass-fronted and padlocked with a large photograph of a man. Below was a notice: *Recuerdo a mi Querido,* and the usual vase of flowers.

But Sigbjørn found the prize: a building as large as a small house but open at the sides, a glass roof like a greenhouse covered with flaking green paint. But the structure itself was made of millions of tiny mirrors cut in every geometrical shape and fitted together in intricate mosaic patterns, balustrade, pillars, down sides like a green temple, even a huge jardinière containing flowering plants, and in the centre of the building a crypt, also covered with mirrors. The whole great thing glittered and flashed in the sun and looked like some M.G.M. set for the Ziegfeld Follies. It was meticulously cared for: someone had even been watering the garden set inside the back of the place, but on one side were an empty tequila bottle, old rags, tin cans, even a broken basket — Sigbjørn remembered that it was waving a tequila bottle from a station platform in Parián that he had last seen Fernando. Ah, poor humanity. The blue painted stucco monuments — the man asleep by a grave — the old building like a grandstand in the cemetery, the sign outside — 'It is forbidden to ride bicycles in the cemetery.' Was Fernando buried in a place like this?

The gigantic tragedy of life goes too fast for those who must merely sit down on some tomb and between scenes try and interpret it, especially when they themselves are actors: Villahermosa! Sigbjørn thought of the loneliness of that death. Un hombre le mató. Perhaps a cold wind blew in Villahermosa as Fernando walked with his high long swift unsteady step, his western tasselled jacket open with the tassels blowing, on his way to that last final cantina, through the high dark night wind — passing through the squares perhaps at night with their uncertain wavering lights, and the wind-blown raucous music from the loudspeakers, the queerly-named popcorn wagons, and the merry-go-rounds empty, perhaps newly painted that morning, under the dark waving trees, the lights were going out one by one, and then one red light glowing by some new road, and beyond the brilliant light of that last fatal cantina, past which two men were urging forward their mules with milk cans, and Fernando moving in step to this sad music through this darkness made for drunkards . . .

Before dinner, tired as they were, they set out for the Santuaria de la Soledad. They passed the closed and dark green Ejidal. They passed Cervantes' Farmacia de la Soledad. They entered the church of the Soledad. A service was going on. The priest was intoning: everyone was saying: 'Santa Maria, madre de Dios, ruega por nosotros pecadores, ahora y en la hora de nuestra muerte, amen. Santa Maria, madre de Dios, ruega por . . . ' Pray for us sinners now and at the hour of our death. Pray for us sinners now and at the hour of our death.'

EXTRACTS BY MALCOLM LOWRY TAKEN FROM:

UNDER THE VOLCANO. *Reprinted by Penguin Books. London, 1985.*
DARK AS THE GRAVE WHEREIN MY FRIEND IS LAID. *Reprinted by Penguin Books. London, 1988.*
SELECTED POEMS OF MALCOLM LOWRY. Edited by Earle Birney with the assistance of Margerie Bonner Lowry. *City Lights Books. San Francisco, 1985.*

FURTHER READING:

MALCOLM LOWRY: A BIOGRAPHY Douglas Day. *Oxford University Press. London, 1974.*
SELECTED LETTERS OF MALCOLM LOWRY Edited by Harvey Breit and Margerie Bonner Lowry. *Penguin Books. London, 1985.*

TWO POEMS BY MALCOLM LOWRY

EPITAPH

Malcolm Lowry
Late of the Bowery
His prose was flowery
And often glowery
He lived, nightly, and drank, daily,
And died playing the ukulele.

FOR THE LOVE OF DYING

The tortures of hell are stern, their fires burn fiercely.
Yet vultures turn against the air more beautifully
than seagulls float downwind in cool sunlight,
or fans in asylums spin a loom of fate
for hope which never ventured up so high
as life's deception, astride the vulture's flight.
If death can fly, just for the love of flying,
What might not life do, for the love of dying?

'Day of the Dead in the Country', Diego Rivera (charcoal, chalk and pencil) 1925. Museum of Moderr Art, New York.

ORIGIN

ROSARIO CASTELLANOS

Over the dead body of a woman I am growing,
on her bones my roots are coiled
and from her disfigured heart
emerges a hard, vertical stalk.
From the coffin of an unborn child:
from its stomach shattered before the harvest
I rise up, tenacious, definitive,
brutal as a gravestone and on occasion sad
with the stony weariness of a funeral angel
who hides a tearless visage beneath his hands.

Translated by Julian Palley
From MEDITATION ON THE THRESHOLD,
Bilingual Press, Tempe, Arizona, 1988

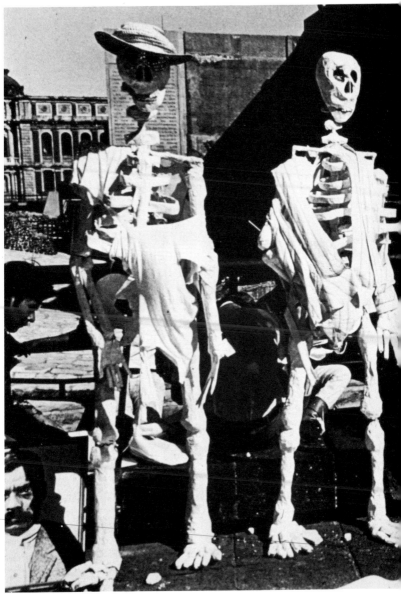

Mexico City offerings for the Day of the Dead. PHOTOGRAPH: YOLANDA ANDRADE.

THE MAGICAL CYCLE OF DAYS

ANTONIO SALVIDAR AND ABRAHAM MAURICIO SALAZAR

IN SAN AUGUSTÍN there are some five or six bakers who make salt bread all the year round and sometimes sweet bread as well. They sell them in the village and to other villages nearby. For the festivals of All Saints and All Souls the making of bread takes on a ritual character which is very important for all villagers. Two or three days before celebrations begin, families make bread figures in the style of angels and human beings; they also fashion round breads which they call *tortas*. On the last day of October, very early, all the children gather in the church; from there they go to the graveyard accompanied by a prayer-maker and by some women; they carry a banner with the image of the Eucharist, bread angels and green branches. The music of the band goes with them. In the graveyard they say some prayers; then they return to the church, symbolically taking the dead children with them. There they pray a second time. Afterwards they go to their houses, where their parents are waiting; they have killed chickens and have cooked *mole* and *tamales* as a vow or offering. This also includes bread, squash, fruits, pumpkin prepared with brown sugar, maize cobs and other foods. When night comes four dishes are laid on the floor of the house, together with candles, flowers and other foodstuffs. The bread and the fruit are kept apart on a little 'sun-and-water' bed made from maize stalks. Family members position candles and tiny angels on top of the dry stone walls or fences, so that the village children can come by and take them. All this makes for great merriment. During the night precautions are taken to stop the animals coming in to eat the offering. Next morning the family eats it and prepares another, this time for the dead adults who also receive prayers. On the third day the children, with the prayer-maker and the band, accompany the dead back to the graveyard. In this way, year after year, the ancient alliance is renewed between the

Vow in the graveyard. Drawing done in black ink on bark paper by Abraham Mauricio Salazar in the village of San Augustin Oapan, Guerrero.

living and the dead; during these days they accompany, support and console one another.

When our road is run, when death puts an end to joys and sorrows, relatives and friends carry the weary body to its final resting place. Those who remain in the world of the living perpetuate the rhythmic cycle ordained by festivals, work and journeys, in San Augustín. It is the flame which endures, it is the weft thread which traverses the magical succession of days.

Written in Spanish by Antonio Saldivar, and translated by Chloë Sayer. Both the text and the drawing by Abraham Mauricio Salazar are from EL CICLO MÁGICO DE LOS DÍAS. *Consejo Nacional de Fomento Educativo, Mexico City, 1985.*

THE JOURNEY OF THE SOUL

EXTRACT FROM *THE ZINACANTECOS OF MEXICO*

EVON Z. VOGT

The Zinacantecos are Maya Indians who speak Tzotzil and live in the highlands of Chiapas. Spanish-Catholic teachings have not erased earlier beliefs and practices. The world is visualised as a cube; above and below are the sky (Vinahel) and the Lower World. Although Zinacantecos revere the Catholic Saints, they believe in several ancient gods; the Earth Owner controls the elements, the land and its produce. The term 'Ladinos', used below, is applied in this region to non-Indians. Evon Z. Vogt has written extensively about indigenous culture in Chiapas.

IN ZINACANTECO belief, no death, even for the very old, results from natural illness in the way in which we consider the process physiologically. Rather, death results from 'soul loss', by having one's animal spirit companion let out of its corral, or by having one's 'inner soul' sold irrevocably to the Earth-Owner; or death may result from physical injury.

Most Zinacantecos die on their reed sleeping mats on the earthen floors of their homes. When death comes, the kerchief of a man, or shawl of a woman, is used to cover the face of the deceased. An older man or woman is called upon to bathe the corpse and dress it in clean clothes. The corpse is then put in a pine coffin, purchased from Ladino carpenters. The head is placed to the West, and a chicken head is put in a bowl of broth beside the head of the corpse, along with some tortillas. The chicken allegedly leads the 'inner soul' of the deceased to *Vinahel*. A black dog carries the 'soul' across a river, and the tortillas compensate the dog for his assistance. Three small bags of money are placed with the body, two of them hidden at the sides so they will not be stolen by the other 'souls' upon arrival in *Vinahel*. At the foot, a small bowl and a gourd with water provide the necessary drinking implements, and a sack of charred tortillas for food for the 'soul' on its journey. Candles are lighted, musicians (violin, harp, guitar) play, and there is an all-night wake for the deceased.

At dawn a ritual meal is served, and preparations are made for the trip to the cemetery. All in the house cry openly to express their grief. The coffin is closed and carried outside where it is fastened to two long poles which will rest on the shoulders of the four pall-bearers who carry it to the cemetery. Since the 'soul' of the deceased wishes to take its family, friends, and possessions along, an important ritual act is performed to protect the survivors, the widow (or widower) spits salt water on the spot where the coffin was located during the wake and at all places around the house and patio where the deceased has worked, walked and slept during his life.

To the accompaniment of loud wailing, the procession now forms, led by the musicians, and proceeds to the cemetery. It stops at specified places along the trail, where the coffin is opened, candles are lighted, prayers are said, and an old woman gives water to the corpse by sprinkling it on the lips with a geranium.

Upon arrival at the cemetery, the coffin is set down and the grave is dug. About every half hour, the deceased is given another drink of water with a red geranium to relieve his thirst. The children who are present step up to the open coffin and kick the side of the coffin so that the deceased will not take their 'souls' with him.

After a final round of prayers, the coffin is closed for the last time, and lowered halfway into the grave, and a round of liquor is served. The coffin is then lowered all the way, and all present come forward to throw three handfuls of dirt over the coffin to prevent the deceased from taking their 'souls'. The hat and high-backed sandals of a man are buried above the coffin, but the black bands in the hat are ripped and the 'ears' of sandals cut — to prevent them from turning into snakes and bull horns. The grave is then completely filled. Fresh pine needles are placed over the grave, a small wooden cross erected at the head (the corpse is buried with its head to the West), and candles are lighted — two white wax and one tallow — in the pit at the head of the grave. The white candles represent tortillas for the 'soul' of the deceased; the tallow candle symbolizes meat.

Interaction with the dead by no means ceases after burial takes place. The close survivors make daily trips to the cemetery for nine days thereafter, following the Catholic 'novena'. Candles are lighted and prayers said. In addition, special rituals are performed on Todos Santos when the graves of all remembered deceased relatives are decorated with fresh pine needles (on the mounds) and pine boughs and red geraniums (on the crosses). The graves are also decorated, prayers said, and candles offered on each important ceremonial occasion, such as the Fiestas of San Lorenzo and San Sebastián. By these ritual means the 'inner soul' of the deceased continues to participate in the fiestas he enjoyed so much during his lifetime.

From: THE ZINACANTECOS OF MEXICO—A MODERN MAYA WAY OF LIFE. Evon Z. Vogt. *Holt, Rinehart & Winston. New York, 1970*

FURTHER READING:
Guiteras-Holmes, Calixta. PERILS OF THE SOUL: THE WORLD VIEW OF A TZOTZIL INDIAN. *The Free Press of Glencoe. New York, 1961.*
Morris Jr., Walter F. LIVING MAYA. *Harry N. Abrahams, Inc. New York, 1987.*
Vogt, Evon Z. ZINACANTAN: A MAYA COMMUNITY IN THE HIGHLANDS OF CHIAPAS. *Harvard University Press. Cambridge, Mass., 1969.*

RIGHT: Aztec carving of Coatlicue, the earth goddess, c. 1500. She is shown with two snake heads; she wears a skirt of writhing snakes, and a necklace of human hearts and hands with a skull. Engraving by Carlos Nebel, published in 'Voyage pittoresque et archéologique dans la partie plus intéressante du Mexique'. Paris, 1836. Courtesy British Library Board.

OVERLEAF: Coatlicue. PHOTOGRAPH: MANUEL ALVAREZ BRAVO

DEATH THE MIRROR

EXTRACT FROM *THE LABYRINTH OF SOLITUDE*

OCTAVIO PAZ

Born in Mexico City in 1914, Octavio Paz is recognized as one of the major poets of our time. He has published more than twenty volumes of poetry and several collections of essays. EL LABERINTO DE LA SOLEDAD first appeared in 1959, and has since been translated into many languages. In these essays Paz reflects on Mexican society and culture, with its 'secret roots' which stretch back far in time. The following is taken from the chapter entitled *Todos santos, día de muertos* (All Saints, Day of the Dead).

THE SOLITARY MEXICAN loves fiestas and public gatherings. Any occasion for getting together will serve, any pretext to stop the flow of time and commemorate men and events with festivals and ceremonies. We are a ritual people, and this characteristic enriches both our imaginations and our sensibilities, which are equally sharp and alert. The art of the fiesta has been debased almost everywhere else, but not in Mexico. There are few places in the world where it is possible to take part in a spectacle like our great religious fiestas with their violent primary colours, their bizarre costumes and dances, their fireworks and ceremonies, and their inexhaustible welter of surprises: the fruit, candy, toys and other objects sold on these days in the plazas and open-air markets.

Our poverty can be measured by the frequency and luxuriousness of our holidays. Wealthy countries have very few: there is neither the time nor the desire for them, and they are not necessary. The people have other things to do, and when they amuse themselves they do so in small groups. The modern masses are agglomerations of solitary individuals. On great occasions in Paris or New York, when the populace gathers in the squares or stadiums, the absence of people, in the sense of *a* people, is remarkable: there are couples and small groups, but they never form a living community in which the individual is at once dissolved and redeemed. But how could a poor Mexican live without the two or three annual fiestas that make up for his poverty and misery? Fiestas are our only luxury. They replace, and are perhaps better than, the theatre and vacations, Anglo-Saxon weekends and cocktail parties, the bourgeois reception, the Mediterranean café.

In all of these ceremonies — national or local, trade or family — the Mexican opens out. They all give him a chance to reveal himself and to converse with God, country, friends or relations. During these days the silent Mexican whistles, shouts, sings, shoots off fireworks, discharges his pistol into the air. He discharges his soul. And his shout, like the rockets we love so much, ascends to the heavens, explodes into green, red, blue and white lights, and falls dizzily to earth with a trail of golden sparks . . .

According to the interpretation of French sociologists, the fiesta is an excess, an expense. By means of this squandering the community protects itself against the envy of the gods or of men. Sacrifices and offerings placate or buy off the gods and the patron saints. Wasting money and expending energy affirms the community's wealth in both. This luxury is a proof of health, a show of abundance and power. Or a magic trap. For squandering is an effort to attract abundance by contagion . . . The fiesta's function, then, is more utilitarian than we think: waste attracts or promotes wealth, and is an investment like any other, except that the returns on it cannot be measured or counted. What is sought is potency, life, health. In this sense the fiesta, like the gift and the offering, is one of the most ancient of economic forms.

This interpretation has always seemed to me to be incomplete. The fiesta is by nature sacred, literally or figuratively, and above all it is the advent of the unusual. It is governed by its own special rules, that set it apart from other days, and it has a logic, an ethic and even an economy that are often in conflict with everyday norms. It all occurs in an enchanted world: time is transformed to a mythical past or a total present; space, the scene of the fiesta, is turned into a fairly decorated world of its own; and the persons taking part cast off all human or social rank and become, for the moment, living images. And everything takes place as if it were not so, as if it were a dream. But whatever happens, our actions have a greater lightness, a different gravity. They take on other meanings and with them we contract new obligations. We throw down our burdens of time and reason.

It is significant that a country as sorrowful as ours should have so many and such joyous fiestas. Their frequency, their brilliance and excitement, the enthusiasm with which we take part, all suggest that without them we would explode. They free us, if only momentarily, from the thwarted impulses, the inflammable desires that we carry within us. But the Mexican fiesta is not merely a return to an original state of formless and normless liberty: the Mexican is not seeking to return, but to escape from himself, to exceed himself. Our fiestas are explosions. Life and death, joy and sorrow, music and mere noise are united, not to re-create or recognize themselves, but to swallow each other up. There is nothing so joyous as a Mexican fiesta, but there is also nothing so sorrowful. Fiesta night is also a night of mourning.

Death is a mirror which reflects the vain gesticulations of the living. The whole motley confusion of acts, omissions, regrets and hopes which is the life of each one of us finds in death, not meaning or explanation, but an end. Death defines life; a death depicts a life in immutable forms; we do not change except to disappear. Our deaths illuminate our lives. If our deaths lack meaning, our lives also lacked it. Therefore we are apt to say, when somebody has died a violent death, 'He got what he was looking for'. Each of us dies the death he is looking for, the death he has made for himself. A Christian death or a dog's death are ways of dying that reflect ways of living. If death betrays us and we die badly, everyone laments the fact, because we should die as we have lived. Death, like life, is not transferable. If we do not die as we lived, it is because the life we lived was not really ours: it did not belong to us, just as the bad death that kills us does not belong to us. Tell me how you die and I will tell you who you are.

The opposition between life and death was not so absolute to the ancient Mexicans as it is to us. Life extended into death, and vice versa. Death was not the natural end of life but one phase of an infinite cycle.

Life, death and resurrection were stages of a cosmic process which repeated itself continuously. Life had no higher function than to flow into death, its opposite and complement; and death, in turn, was not an end in itself: man fed the insatiable hunger of life with his death. Sacrifices had a double purpose: on the one hand man participated in the creative process, at the same time paying back to the gods the debt contracted by his species; on the other hand he nourished cosmic life and also social life, which was nurtured by the former.

Perhaps the most characteristic aspect of this conception is the impersonal nature of the sacrifice. Since their lives did not belong to them, their deaths lacked any personal meaning. The death — including warriors killed in battle and women dying in childbirth, companions of Huitzilopochtli the sun god — disappeared at the end of a certain period, to return to the undifferentiated country of the shadows, to be melted into the air, the earth, the fire, the animating substance of the universe. Our indigenous ancestors did not believe that their deaths belonged to them, just as they never thought that their lives were really theirs in the Christian sense. Everything was examined to determine, from birth, the life and death of each man: his social class, the year, the place, the day, the hour. The Aztec was as little responsible for his actions as for his death.

The advent of Catholicism radically modified this situation. Sacrifice and the idea of salvation, formerly collective, became personal. Freedom was humanized, embodied in man. To the ancient Aztecs the essential thing was to assure the continuity of creation; sacrifice did not bring about salvation in another world, but cosmic health; the universe, and not the individual, was given life by the blood and death of human beings. For Christians it is the individual who counts. The world — history, society — is condemned beforehand. The death of Christ saved each man in particular. Each one of us is Man, and represents the hopes and possibilities of the species. Redemption is a personal task.

Both attitudes, opposed as they may seem, have a common note: life, collective or individual, looks forward to a death that in its way is a new life. Life only justifies and transcends itself when it is realized in death, and death is also a transcendence, in that it is a new life. To Christians death is a transition, a somersault between two lives, the temporal and the other-worldly; to the Aztecs it was the profoundest way of participating in the continuous regeneration of the creative forces, which were always in danger of being extinguished if they were not provided with blood, the sacred food. In both systems life and death lack autonomy, are the two sides of a single reality. They are references to the invisible realities.

Modern death does not have any significance that transcends it or that refers to other values. It is rarely anything more than the inevitable conclusion of a natural process. In a world of facts, death is merely one more fact. But since it is such a disagreeable fact, contrary to all our concepts and to the very meaning of our lives, the philosophy of progress ('Progress towards what, and from what?' Scheler asked) pretends to make it disappear, like a magician palming a coin. Everything in the modern world functions as if death did not exist. Nobody takes it into account, it is suppressed everywhere: in political pronouncements, commercial advertising, public morality and popular customs; in the promise of cut-rate health and happiness offered to all of us by hospitals, drugstores and playing fields. But death enters into everything we undertake, and it is no longer a transition but a great gaping mouth that nothing can satisfy.

Death also lacks meaning for the modern Mexican. It is no longer a transition, an access to another life more alive than our own. But although we do not view death as a transcendence, we have not eliminated it from our daily lives. The word death is not pronounced in New York, in Paris, in London, because it burns the lips. The Mexican, in contrast, is familiar with death, jokes about it, caresses it, sleeps with it, celebrates it; it is one of his favourite toys and his most steadfast love. True, there is perhaps as much fear in his attitude as in that of others, but at least death is not hidden away: he looks at it face to face, with impatience, disdain or irony. 'If they are going to kill me tomorrow, let them kill me right away.'*

*From the popular folk song *La Valentina* — *Translator.*

The Mexican's indifference towards death is fostered by his indifference towards life. He views not only death but also life as non-transcendent. Our songs, proverbs, fiestas and popular beliefs show very clearly that the reason death cannot frighten us is that 'life has cured us of fear'. It is natural, even desirable, to die, and the sooner the better. We kill because life — our own or another's — is of no value. Life and death are inseparable, and when the former lacks meaning, the latter becomes equally meaningless. Mexican death is the mirror of Mexican life. And the Mexican shuts himself away and ignores both of them.

Our contempt for death is not at odds with the cult we have made of it. Death is present in our fiestas, our games, our loves and our thoughts. To die and to kill are ideas that rarely leave us. We are seduced by death. The fascination it exerts over us is the result, perhaps, of our hermit-like solitude and of the fury with which we break out of it. The pressure of our vitality, which can only express itself in forms that betray it, explains the deadly nature, aggressive or suicidal, of our explosions. When we explode we touch against the highest point of that tension, we graze the very zenith of life. And there, at the height of our frenzy, suddenly we feel dizzy: it is then that death attracts us.

Another factor is that death revenges us against life, strips it of all its vanities and pretensions and converts it into what it really is: a few neat bones and a dreadful grimace. In a closed world where everything is death, only death has value. But our affirmation is negative. Sugar-candy skulls, and tissue-paper skulls and skeletons strung with fireworks . . . our popular images always poke fun at life, affirming the nothingness and insignificance of human existence. We decorate our houses with death's heads, we eat bread in the shape of bones on the Day of the Dead, we love the songs and stories in which death laughs and cracks jokes, but all this boastful familiarity does not rid us of the question we all ask: What is death? We have not thought up a new answer. And each time we ask, we shrug our shoulders: Why should I care about death if I have never cared about life?

Extract taken from THE LABYRINTH OF SOLITUDE: LIFE AND THOUGHT IN MEXICO
Translated by Lysander Kemp. *Allen Lane The Penguin Press, 1967*

OVERLEAF: PHOTOGRAPH: MANUEL ALVAREZ BRAVO.

CAJAS

MORTUORIAS